BANDITRY REGIME

Galadima Bitrus

BANDITRY REGIME

By

GALADIMA BITRUS

ISBN: 9798807763655

Copyright © 2022 Galadima Bitrus

All Enquiries To
+234 (0)903 405 3324

Designed, by
DgalaGraphiz
Email: dgala0019@gmail.com
+234 (0)8147163578
+234 (0)7052404294

FOREWORD!

I count it a great privilege to be asked by the author of this incredibly amazing piece: 'Banditry Regime' Galadima Bitrus; to write the foreword. Accept my sincere congratulations for this giant intellectual work.

My first impression on this book is the sincerity and impartiality mixed with the manly boldness exhibited by Galadima in his writings. It is what it is and nothing more pretentious. Without mincing words, the author in a lucid, fluent and manifestly eloquent prose; spared no time in clearing his mind on the subject devoid of any form of decoration or some sort of unhealthy political criticisms or personal attack which would perhaps be perceived as either soliciting for a favour of any kind. Instead, he hinged consistently on his neutrality and the essence of the piece which captures the sad but candid reality of our existence.

Without fear of contradiction, the author took his time with enormous industry to carefully elaborate succinctly on the types of Governments as postulated by various proponents and or great philosophers prior to our time. Given us an acute background on each. He then went on to introduce the particular and peculiar one which none of the great philosophers ever envisioned, "Banditry Regime."

Haven talked expansively on plethora of Governments/regimes, a brilliant analysis on the vices that begot our current nightmare ensued. There's no gain attempting to conceal for whatever reason, the fact that the response and attitudes of the Government officials on this trend gave birth to this unspeakable horror, horror so terrific that is blazing energetically to consume us. The author left no stone unturned in this regard.

The in-depth analysis and collation of security/insecurity reports as reported by major Newspaper outlets across the whole country, the North and Niger State precisely is the testament that the author of this book has unraveled.

A very pathetic and unfortunate incident that has eaten deep into our system as a result of poor and atrocious leadership, consequently exposing and endangering the lives and properties of innocent citizens. May I further state affirmatively that it is the responsibility of the Government globally both democratically and constitutionally to ensure that "absolute security" of the lives and properties of it's citizens is guaranteed. This book has further revealed how the actors have failed woefully including how the system is now nothing more or less than an "acephalous" society.

Let me emphasize on the chapters dealing with "Outsider's report (Sieved, Refined and Polished)/Insider's report (Unsieved, Unrefined and Unpolished)". The book offered tremendously on the truth, and the throe of our people, our true story. You'll agree with the author that we have never had it this bad. It therefore boils down to the inadequacies and dilapidation of the security infrastructures that has been put in place from time immemorial with a very infinitesimal or no positive outcome. The bandits keeps staging series of attacks on innocent citizens and nothing has ever been done either to defuse the attacks, protect the citizens or to assuage subsequent attack. No measures at all.

I wasted no time aligning myself with the submission of the author that Banditry is an agency of the Government of the day, given their antics, well and tactically organized modules operand. One could easily be convinced that in other to clear the coast for the bandits to unleash their terror on the harmless and helpless citizens, the little security outfit gets withdrawn or recalled; leaving the villagers to perish, eliminating even the slightest hope of repelling any possible attack. Do we have an army of our own to defend us? The answer is in the negative. Our little flame of hope is blown away, it metamorphoses into a devastating horror, with women and children right in the middle of this catastrophic experience. Sad indeed! This book is rich, accurate and concise, in that it encapsulates most of the tragic events both past and present in Nigeria, the North Central, Niger State and in Adunu (our hometown).

Banditry Regime is not a fictitious prose that aims at satisfying your leisure, it is the true account of the terror and horror that caught us unprepared, our true sad story.

I find this piece quite useful and exquisite to myself and

other lay readers who also crave for the enlightenment embedded herein. It is unique, educative and informative replete with wisdom for a keen reader. It can never be easy to sufficiently congratulate Mr. Galadima Bitrus once again for this stunning achievement. May I further stress my ardent recommendation to the readers of this amazing piece.

Clinton Daniels Esq.,

21st April, 2022

DEDICATION

I dedicate this book to countless friends, relatives, the known and unknown people of Adunu, Gwada, Ishau, Dakalo, Amale, Sarkin-Powa, Daza, Feri, Barakwai, Kushiri, Tungan Barau and Beni suffocated by the thick smoke of this new but fierce and wild regime prevailing in Nigeria.

We are right here still looking up and down for where the answer to our deepest heart cry (How long will this regime reign before we find deliverance?) will come. You nurtured these questions too, and I am in tears telling you we are yet to find an answer to the most frequent question on your lips before your forceful elimination.

CONTENTS

ACKNOWLEDGMENTS

I am a man indebted to my local community (Adunu) and its environs, it made me what I am today and I'm not ashamed of you — my home! It gave me the geographical and mental standpoint that enabled me have this unique view of the trend of things in the inside of northern Nigeria (North Central to be precise).

Your forward to this book Barrister Clinton Daniels is a voice that cannot be silenced, thanks for giving me your seal.
Z. B. Yilkes and B. G. Dauda made it possible for this book to reach you in this form, take my salute friends!

Finally, to my wife and Son, G. B. Gift and O. B. Augustine (Galadima Jr.) I am sure they are happy now for what they sacrificed for is achieved.

1 CHAPTER

FORMS OF REGIMES

I write to you from a remote area in the North central part of Nigeria (Adunu in Paikoro Local Government Area to be precise).
You might have read of the many forms of regimes this world has witnessed. But I want to tell you of this very one regime that neither Plato nor any great philosopher ever mentioned nor described.

Regime Defined
An online publisher1 have this to say about the word "Regime"; "system of government or rule, mode of management," "rule, guidance, government, means of guidance, rudder", could also mean "to direct, to guide" "to direct in a straight line," thus "to lead, rule".

This led to the conventional definition that the word regime refers to the organization that is the governing authority of a political unit.
That is, a regime is the way and the mechanism that remotes a set. It is a way of reigning to which everyone and everything must submit to. It essentially refers to a mode or system of a government, or simply a ruling government of the country.

A brief look on the known regimes mentioned and explained in the write-ups of many Philosophers, Politicians, and regime analysts reveals the following forms of regime:

they are aristocracy, timocracy, oligarchy, democracy, and tyranny (Plato's five regimes), and lots of others from different thinkers and observers.

1. Aristocracy

Aristocracy is the form of government (politeia) advocated in Plato's Republic. The regime is ruled by a philosopher king, and thus is grounded on wisdom and reason. It is composed of three caste-like parts: the ruling class, made up of the aforementioned philosopher-kings; the auxiliaries of the ruling caste, made up of soldiers, and whose job in the state is to force on the majority the order established by the philosophers; and the majority of the people, who, in contrast to the first two classes, are allowed to own property and produce goods for themselves, but are also obliged to sustain with their own activities their rulers'.

2. Timocracy

Timocracy, in choosing its leaders, is "inclining rather to the more high-spirited and simple-minded type, who are better suited for war".[1] The governors of timocracy value power, which they seek to attain primarily by means of military conquest and the acquisition of honors, rather than intellectual means. Plato characterizes timocracy as a mixture of the elements of two different regime types — aristocracy and oligarchy.

3. Oligarchy

It is a system of government which distinguishes between the rich and the poor, making out of the former its administrators.

An oligarchy is originated by extending tendencies already evident in a timocracy. In contrast to Platonic aristocrats, timocrats are allowed by their constitution to own property and thus to both accumulate and waste money. Because of the pleasures derived therefrom, money eventually is prized over virtue, and the leaders of the state seek to alter the law to give way and accommodate to the materialistic lust of its citizens. As a result of this newfound appreciation for money, the governors rework the constitution yet again to restrict political power to the rich only. That is how a timocracy becomes an oligarchy.

4. Democracy

Democracy is the end product of a degenerated oligarchy system of government where freedom is the supreme good but freedom is also slavery. In democracy, the lower class grows bigger and bigger. The poor become the winners. People are free to do what they want and live how they want. People can even break the law if they so choose. This appears to be very similar to anarchy.

Plato used the "democratic man" to represent democracy. The democratic man is the son of the oligarchic man. Unlike his father, the democratic man is consumed with unnecessary desires. Plato describes necessary desires as desires that we have out of instinct or desires that we have to survive. Unnecessary desires are desires we can teach ourselves to resist such as the desire for riches.

The democratic man takes great interest in all the things he can buy with his money. Plato believes that the democratic man is more concerned with his money over how he can help the people. He does whatever he wants whenever he wants to do it. His life has no order or priority.

Plato does not believe that democracy is the best form of government. According to him, equality brings power-seeking individuals who are motivated by personal gain. They can be highly corruptible, and this can eventually lead to tyranny. This form of government is unstable, and it lacks leaders with proper skills and morals. Without able and virtuous leaders, who come and go, it is not a good form of government. He sees democracy as dangerous as it motivates the poor against the wealthy rulers. It prioritizes wealth and property accumulation.[2]

5. Tyranny

When Democracy degenerates, the tyranny regime ensue. Here, no one has discipline and society exists in chaos. Democracy is taken over by the longing for freedom. Power must be seized to maintain order. A champion will come along and experience power, which will cause him to become a tyrant. The people will start to hate him and eventually try to remove him but will realize they are not able.

The tyrannical man is the son of the democratic man. He is the worst form of man due to his being the most unjust and thus the furthest removed from any joy of the true kind. He is consumed by lawless desires which cause him to do many terrible things such as murdering and plundering. He comes closest to complete lawlessness. The idea of moderation does not exist to him. He is consumed by the basest pleasures in life, and being granted these pleasures at a whim destroys the type of pleasure only attainable through knowing pain.

If he spends all of his money and becomes poor, the tyrant will steal and conquer to satiate his desires, but will eventually overreach and force unto himself a fear of those around him, effectively limiting his own freedom. The tyrant always runs the risk of being killed in revenge for all the unjust things he has done. He becomes afraid to leave his own home and becomes trapped inside. Therefore, his lawlessness leads to his own self-imprisonment.

6. Federation

It can be defined as a political organization characterized by the union of small states, groups or parties, which are self-governed in internal affairs and are united under a central government. The division of power among the states and the central governing body is typically constitutionally entrenched. A federal government having the constitutional structure that can be considered the opposite of a unitary state system

7. Theocracy

A government of a state by priests ruling in the name of God or gods, or by officials who are regarded as divinely guided, or consistent with the doctrines and principles of a particular religion or religious community. There is little room for dissent as the divine order is considered unquestionable and absolute.

8. Communism

Derived from the French Commune (common), it is a revolutionary socialist movement aimed at creating a classless society that abolishes private ownership. The property is held by the community rather than the individuals and all activity is controlled by the government. As a system of government, communism is often closer to a form of socialism, in which the state owns and operates industry on behalf of the people.

9. Republic

Republic is a government whose authority is based on citizen voters, which are represented by elected or nominated officials chosen in free elections, as opposed to a monarchy or a dictatorship where the supreme power lies with the ruler.

10. Totalitarian

Easy to decipher from the 'total'; a totalitarian system is the one in which a single political authority regulates total control over the state that is centralized and dictatorial. It advocates complete subservience to the political authority which controls.

11. Cabal

Derived from Kaballah, a philosophy which is an integral part of Judaism; rather than being a form of government, a cabal is a group of people or a plot by a group of people to promote their interests in a community or state, usually sinister ones. The term today has an association with shadowy corners, black rooms or secretive government affairs.

12. Junta

Having its origin from Spanish word Junta, which has its roots in Latin jungere (to join). It refers to a group or coalition that takes control of the state after overthrowing a government. Usually, this is done by military groups and the rule established is tightly controlled.

13. Dictatorship

Originally, a reference to a temporary emergency government established by the Roman Senate, dictatorship today refers to a form of government or social situation where the power rests entirely on one person or a group of persons. This rule could be acquired by inheritance or force and is usually oppressive, with no regulation by constitution, laws or opposition.

14. Authoritarian

Beginning with the Latin word 'author', meaning teacher or master, it is more of a description than being an actual form of government. A rule characteristic of a ruler having absolute sovereignty and centralized/highly concentrated power maintained by political repression can be termed as authoritarian. The term can also be used to connote arbitrary law situation such as election rigging or decisions made behind closed doors by a select group of government members.

15. Autocracy

Coming from Greek roots 'auto' meaning self and 'kratos' meaning power, the word autocracy refers to a government controlled by absolute power, concentrated in the hands of a single person with minimal restraints on the decisions and lack of any regularized mechanisms of popular control.

16. Fascism

Having taken a different form, fascism has evolved dramatically in various ways over the years. It is a way of ruling that advocates total control of the people and seeks to promote the ancestral and cultural values and eradicate foreign influences that are deemed to cause degeneration to the national and moral values of the people.

17. Plutocracy

The Greek word 'ploutos' means wealth, so plutocracy is a government ruled by the rich or power provided by wealth. It can also be used to describe a wealthy class ruling a government, often from behind the scenes.

18. Technocracy

As the name suggests, technocracy is a form of government where scientists and technical experts are in control of the state. Initially used to designate the application of scientific method to solving social problems, the term now is used for a rule where rulers are selected on the basis of their knowledge and skill rather than wealth or power.

19. Unitary

A unitary state is the one characterized by or constituting a form of government in which power is held by one central authority, and the administrative divisions can only exercise those powers that the central authority chooses to delegate. A great number of nations have this form of government.

20. Banditry Regime

It is not defined here. Please read on to find out this one peculiar regime that neither Plato nor the teacher in the classroom ever mentioned.

2 CHAPTER

BANDITRY REGIME

No human so humane enough will not stop by to give this new trend a consideration. You need to know that I am not speaking from a politician's point of view, I'm not trying to promote one administration over another.

This book is not one of the many books engineered to buttress the defamation campaign of administrations by many power-hungry individuals seizing the sorry happenings in lovely Nigeria to promote their personal interest.

This is just a description of a regime at work in Nigeria that no one has taken time to include it in the ever growing and dynamic list of regimes witnessed over time.

And so, you need to sit tight, and read keenly to be sure you get this definition that no other book than this can give.

The word Banditry stemmed from the word bandit. A bandit is a "lawless robber, brigand" (especially as part of an organized band). It is one who is considered an "outlaw,". That is, an individual who has done something illegal and is hiding to avoid been caught; a person not protected by the law.

We can say that a bandit is one whose doings are "proscribed, banished and forbidden". May be, you had never personally encountered a bandit, but as you read of who a bandit is and of such things they can do in this book, I am sure that every idea will give you goose bumps.

Banditry regime is a regime currently practiced in Nigeria. One of Nigeria's promising presidential aspirant for the next general elections (Bola Tinubu) made the front-page headline of major Nigerian newspapers on April 17th, 2022 when he promised to give Nigerians "A Banditry-free, United Nigeria" in one of his campaigns.

In other words, the current Nigeria is plagued with banditry (callous operations of bandits). It means Nigeria is not bandits free — the cankerworm is still there and is even eating deeper by day. I am not painting the nation black, I am just giving an exposé on the statement of this senior statesman.

Banditry regime as practiced in Nigeria is a form of government with a democratically elect representative at all levels of government which shares the national security powers with a sect termed bandit. Yes, the sitting government calls them bandits but they are not.

By name, the government refers to them as bandits but government's action gives an idea that it shares power with this sect. They are not bandits because bandits are people that are outlawed. Bandits are people that are hiding to avoid been caught. They have no protection of the law. But this Nigerian bandit are not hiding, they cannot be caught and are protected by the law more than a decent citizen on the street.

While its twin (the democratical elect representative) stays and functions in political offices in the cities to give the nation a social face to the international world, the sister (bandits) remain in the forests and thick bushes of remote communities of Nigeria to unleash their terror.

The twin sister from the city visits the sister in the forest for a national discourse on decisions and policy making. Banditry is a new arm of the Nigerian forces: Police, Land Army, Air Force, Navy and Bandits.

The police are withdrawn from remote areas and villages of northern Nigeria because bandits are now situated in such places and the government agrees that these bandits become its eye.

These bandits are supplied with sophisticated weapons than even the Soldiers, they are given more law protection than any other arm of Nigerian force. Any citizen or security personnel who kills them is condemned but they can kill as many citizens and other security personnels without any condemnation.

I emphasize, that these bandits carry out their operations in the open, they rustle cattles, kidnap people and demand ransom from their loved ones and even from the government. Police and Soldiers are told to stay out of their way. They bandits now control the airspace of areas under their jurisdiction.

Bandits organized in many bands across the 36 states of the federation including the state capital can be allowed autonomy over land space of 5 to 10 Local Government

Areas (for example, in Niger state; Paikoro, Munya, Suleja, Bida, Kontagora, Kagara, and many other Local Government Areas have been left to them to run "security patrol for the nation", and the go about harassing innocent and decent citizens with no one saying anything.

Banditry regime is a system of government that bears a democratic face having a democratic body but its nature — its soul and spirit is that which favors bandits. It is a form of government where bandits controls the nation even when they are not physically occupying the so called 'seats of power'.

From a distance, you will think it is anarchy but it is not. Anarchy is when everyone is lawless, everyone is allowed to go the way he wished. But this banditry regime is not so. There is law for the decent citizens, except this ruling class that consists of the political office holders and the bandits. It is a glaring unchecked reign of men that ought to be banished, forbidden and proscribed.

In such a regime, the prevailing posture of the government is reactive to one of being proactive. The bandits are leading in the battle while the government security forces are simply reactive, often lethargically and in an uncoordinated way.

Go a step further from here to find varying reports from established sources that add sinews and flesh to your skeletal understanding of this new system of government adopted in Nigeria.

3 CHAPTER

THE OUTSIDER'S REPORT (SIEVED, REFINED AND POLISHED)

Welcome to the outsider's report on the evolution of a new form of government. I prefer given you tidbits of the outsider's report before giving you mine. It will wet your appetite to welcome the insider's report. Perhaps that may fortify my point that this is not an attempt to paint my nation black or criticize any administration.

Remember that the outsider's report is the analysis of a person or people who are not inside. They stand outside to give their own report based on what they heard or were told. They really do not know much because at least, some of them have never personally encountered a formidable team of bandits in operation. How can you describe a shoe better than he whose feet are fettered in it?

If that was the only problem, then I will ask you to trust the exactness of their report to about 45%. But that is not the only short coming of their report. The outsider does not catch a full gist of the whole situation and still makes deliberate attempts to soften its severity to the hearing of those outside especially the international world. I personally feel this single act by those outsiders (whoever they might be) is not polite and an effort to extend the reign of this very government form that has wrecked and is still wrecking many innocent lives.

The outsider's report is first of all sieved and refined, every hard and horrible part of the story that will be hard for you to chew is removed. Their report is again polished to give a good look to the tensed country by suppressing the agonizing cry of innocent and decent citizens. These outsiders call it broadcasting ethics and many other professional titles. This account is not up to 45% of what is really happening.

So, run through this report with patience knowing that it is not half of what happened and is still happening:

Daily Trust Newspaper (3 November, 2021)
The Newspaper captured the Chief Executive Officer of the Nigerian Financial Intelligence Unit (NFIU), Mr Modibbo Tukur, as saying that "Nigeria will no longer experience banditry and kidnapping by April 2022". This was while speaking at a 3-day capacity building workshop on anti-money laundering and combatting the financing of terrorism in Abuja. He assured us that "The terminal date for kidnapping and banditry is March/April 2022."

And so, I want to fetch just a few from the many reports of happenings in the very month he prophesied was going to be the terminal date for kidnapping and banditry in Nigeria. These are sad events that dominated the first half of April 2022.

Vanguard Newspaper (April 11, 2022)
"Over 70 people were confirmed killed in the Sunday afternoon attacks in some communities in the Kanam local government area of Plateau State while yet to be known a number of people sustained injuries.

The affected communities, where the property was also razed are Kukawa, Gyambawu, Dungur, Kyaram, Yelwa, Dadda, Wanka, Shuwaka, Gwammadaji, and Dadin Kowa".

The Guardian Newspaper (April 12, 2022)
Sources from communities in Kanam Local Council of Plateau State claimed that the gunmen that attacked Kukawa, Gyambawu, Dungur, Kyaram, Yelwa, Dadda, Wanka, Shuwaka, Gwamnadaji and Dadin Kowa villages on Sunday killed 78 persons.

According to him, the number of dead bodies in the bush is still unknown, same with the number of houses razed. Another witness, who gave his name as Sariki Bitrus, said that over 70 persons, mostly women and children, were abducted.

Vanguard (April 6, 2022)
Competent military sources confirmed last night that troops of the Nigerian Army, comprising mainly Army Headquarters Garrison and Guards Brigade, have been put on red alert to avert a revenge attack by bandits/terrorists whose members were repelled earlier last week, in a failed attempt to infiltrate the Federal Capital territory through the Suleija/Zuma axis. This is just as it emerged that the death toll of soldiers who were felled by the terrorists in the

ambush attack had risen to 16.

"...cases of kidnapping have been frequent in the FCT, especially in the communities located along the Abuja/Lokoja highways and this necessitated the deployment of troops. "Additionally, you know we are in an election season and criminals would do anything to want to destabilize the relative peace in the nation's capital with their evil activities which they have been trying for some time without success."

"In particular, areas of interest to the military and other security agencies where suspected criminal elements are believed to be hibernating include Zuba, Madalla, Gwagwalada, Bwari, Nyayan, Kugbo, Gwagwa, Mpape, Karmo, Kubwa kuje, Masaka, Apo, Masaka, Gudu as well as some major markets in the city and troops area are taking no chances."

Notice the number of areas around the Federal Capital Territory that these bandits are believed to be lodging. Remember too, that this is just about 45% of the real thing. I hope you also pick that silent but salient point that this happened as the bandits made an attempt to infiltrate the Federal Capital territory through the Suleija/Zuma axis. Infiltrate the Federal Capital Territory (FCT), I hope you know and understand what that means?

The FCT (Abuja) is the safest place in the whole of Nigeria. It harbours the seat of the President of the Federal republic of Nigeria, the vice President and all the members of the Parliament (109 serving Senators and 360 honorable members of the House of Representatives).

This is just to mention but a few of the caliber of people that resides within the FCT where the bandits tried to infiltrate. And remember, that every one of these men mentioned above is given a convoy of heavily armed soldiers and police. This should help your imagination to picture what has been the fate of communities with little to security outpost of any sort.

Let's look at a few more reports just within this year 2022 — January to April (the period of my writing):

Premium Times (January 23, 2022)
At least 486 people were killed in the first three weeks of 2022 by non-state actors across Nigeria, an average of 22 people a day.

Over 80 per cent of the killings were carried out by terror groups that have terrorized the North-west and North-central zones while **about 50 per cent of the total killings occurred in Niger State, North-central Nigeria.**

Bear in mind that this outsider's report is sieved, refined and polished so that it doesn't irritate your ears. Secondly, if about 50% of the killings occurred in Niger state alone, then no one can give you a vivid description of the reign and sovereignty of this new regime than a Nigerlite like me. You need to hear it from the mouth of a Nigerlite who is not under any national band political obligation to sugarcoat whatever news that must ooze out of his belly.

The Conversion (18 April, 2022)

"Currently, bandits operate in many states of northwestern and north-central Nigeria. The critical hotbeds are Zamfara, Katsina, Kebbi, Kaduna, Sokoto, Nasarawa and Niger.

In these states, notorious crimelords and clans of bandits affiliated to them control swathes of rural enclaves. There they've foisted a **regime of brigandage**, and an underground economy based on illicit franchise.

The bandits are getting more audacious and virulent by the day. And they appear to be buoyed by their apparent criminal impunity in the context of a receding state.

CRITICAL HOTBEDS

Currently, bandits operate in many states of northwestern and north-central Nigeria.

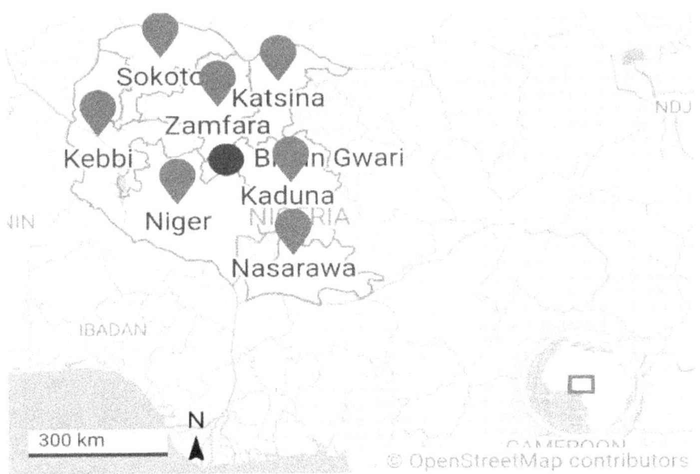

Map: Usifo Omozokpea • Source. Al Chukwuma Okoli • Created with Datawrapper

They have engaged in mass abduction of villagers and school children, attacked markets and raided mines, kidnapped for ransom, as well as carried out highway robberies. They have graduated from attacking vulnerable communities and commuters in the countryside to targeting critical national infrastructures and military facilities in peri-urban areas.

On March 28, 2022 bandits succeeded in demobilizing and attacking a Kaduna-Abuja train after bombing its tracks. The attack underscored not only the intractability of the banditry crisis but also its deteriorating dynamics.

Central and regional governments have responded through a variety of strategies. These have ranged from militarized to non-militarized operations. For example, governments of the affected states have sought to assuage the bandits through peace initiatives and amnesty deals. This has been to no avail.

The publisher has this question to ask:
- How can authorities in Nigeria reposition its fight against banditry in order to ensure greater efficiency?

- What were the challenges of the previously implemented strategies and measures?

- What needs to be done differently?

- Is there any prospects for a more effective counter-**banditry regime** in Nigeria?

The reporter argued that the banditry crisis has festered

owing to the continued decline in the coercive capabilities of the Nigerian state. The crisis has prevailed largely because of the complacency and lethargy with which the Nigerian government has responded to it.

The Vanguard (2 April, 2022)
A group of Civil Society Organizations, CSOs, the Community of Practice Against Mass Atrocities, and the Joint Action Civil Society Committee under the auspices of Nigeria Mourns, Thursday, said that no fewer than 1, 545 Nigerians were killed and 1,321 were abducted by terrorist groups between January 1 and March 30, 2022, a period of 90 days.

Vanguard captioned his report as "INSECURITY: When will Buhari's marching orders end?" This was because the group held that in the last 72 hours the President has issued two orders or directives to security forces on insecurity in the country.

The two orders marked the 28th order President Buhari would be issuing to security chiefs in 35 months. On March 29, the President directed security agencies to ensure that all the passengers that were kidnapped by bandits after attacking the Abuja to Kaduna bound train were rescued

President Buhari also gave a marching order to the security to ensure that each of the callous terrorists that carried out the dastardly act was hunted down and made to face justice for the heinous acts, saying no one or group should be allowed to make the country prostrate.

Few hours after the order, bandits attacked two communities in Giwa LGA of Kaduna State, killing 23 and abducting many people. The point here is that this is usually the case with everyone of the 28th orders. These orders are to give a false sense of concern but in actual sense, 28th orders in 35 months never helped us.

Aljazeera (2 April, 2022)
"Ever since this started, there has not been one single government official that has called any of the family members to say have you heard from family members or to even ask us for intel," she said. "The abductors have reached out to us and [let] our family members speak with [us]. You might expect that this might interest the government right, even [if] they are not going to help us."

This is the voice of a relative of the over 150 passengers missing from the train attack of March 28, 2022. "An answer is all we have always wanted," is their cry.

Premium Times (17 April, 2022)
"Week of Killings: 215 people killed last week across Nigeria, worst in 2022". That's a caption.

The Vanguard (17 April, 2022)
"Bloody Easter in Niger as Bandits kill four, kidnap scores in Gwada Community". What a caption? Read below to ascertain its contents;

"Minna- Bandits have launched a fresh attack on Tafila village, near Gwada town in Shiroro Local government of Niger State with four people reportedly killed and scores abducted. The attack took place at about 6:30 pm on Saturday.

Gwada town which is in Shiroro local government area of the state is about twenty minutes' drive to the multimillion Naira Shiroro Electricity Dam and also about twenty-five kilometers to Minna, the state capital.

Among those killed were two women including two kids of which one of them was the child of one of the deceased women. An eyewitness from the area told our Correspondent that the child was shot in the head and died instantly with the skull scattered.

Our Correspondent also learnt that the Bandits stormed the village on Motorcycles each carrying no fewer than two to three passengers and fully armed with AK47 rifles.

They targeted a truck conveying villagers from Erena town to Gwada where hundreds of IDPs are presently staying and fired bullets at them at close range. Besides those who died, several others in the truck were said to have been seriously injured and are now receiving treatments in various health Centres within the state.

While many of the villagers ran for safety into the bush, many others were unlucky as they ran into the waiting hands of the bandits and were abducted and led into the bush. Many Cattles were also reported to have been rustled by the bandits".

I hope you marked that paragraph above in bold and still remembers that this is just an outsider's report of the situation. A report he/she is mandated by professional ethics to sieve its horror, refine its pain and polish its ugly look to make it presentable.

However, I hope you are able to deduce the sovereign prevalence of this regime (its dominion and power) even from that sieved, refined and polished report.

I can go on and on to give you reports from outsiders but, my heart boils with eagerness to take you to the next chapter on the insider's view, the most essential part of the book. Travel with me to the chapter long awaited for.

4 CHAPTER

THE INSIDER'S REPORT (UNSIEVED, UNREFINED AND UNPOLISHED)

I remind you that I am not doing a defamation campaign against anyone. I am not with any politician neither am I against any of them. This is simply an account of an insider describing a new system of governance witnessed in Nigeria.

There are two (2) ways of viewing media lies in broadcasting and publication;

❖ The first of them is a lie understood as an excess of truthfulness.

❖ The second of them is a lie synonymous with incomplete, limited truthfulness.

I promise to be very careful of all I will say here. I shall not be over zealous and I shall not conceal what you need to know. You may expect a very long discussion here but it will not be so.

To aid my own report in this chapter, (since it is known that sometimes the media is not at liberty and utter independence to say it out the way it happens) I want you to imagine what the real figures of all the killings captured in Chapter 3 will be.

Like I said before, those reports from reputable media outlets were sieved and refined to ensure that they don't aggravate sarcasm and loss of confidence on the Nigerian state. I also hope you took note that none of those reports came from unreliable sources. They are not excerpts from the post of angry citizens thoughtlessly pushed to the Facebook, Instagram or Twitter world.

All I hope to tell you in this chapter is that there is a free reign of a banditry dynasty in this country. That is what I also aimed at telling throughout the chapters you travelled through above.

Pay attention to this brief story of what is going on in some parts of Niger state:
Growing up as little kids in a village, whenever we hear the sound of an aeroplane even at very high altitudes, we rush out to the open space to catch a gaze of the plane. The joy on our face is usually immeasurable, we were always glad to hear the sound of a plane.

We rejoiced greatly at the sight of an aeroplane even in the sky because none of us had ever seen or touched an Aeroplane in the airport. Much of the details we know about Aeroplanes, Jets and Helicopters smelled from the many American films we watched.

If you want to see adults and children stopping whatever they are doing and running to the open field gazing upwards, cause an Helicopter to fly at a very low altitude. That was how we lived before, the sight of a plane in the space gladdened our hearts.

However, reverse is now the case. Currently, the sound or sight of plane especially a Helicopter flying over our space causes great fear, panic and an expectation of woe. This all began when two years back, we noticed that anytime this particular Helicopter flies over our space towards the thick forests around us (Sarkin-powa axis), bandits will storm our axis; raid villages, rustle large herd of cattle, abduct many people and do many more horrible things.

It started that way as a mere assumption until our assumption became established when that happening became consistent. Local intelligence revealed that the Helicopter serve to supply ammunitions to the bandits lodging in the forest.

The Helicopter saga continued until recently when that very Helicopter began patrolling our space. It was then we knew that bandits rule this nation. They control our airspace. The Helicopter flies at very low altitudes to check regions and spots with teeming herd of Cattle.

This same Helicopter remain in the space while this criminal element carries out their operations on the land. That is, it serves to offer the bandits a backup should there be any powerful interference.

Gone are the days when cattle rearing Fulanis dominated

our grasslands peacefully. We cohabited peacefully with them, Cattle dung from their herds was a manure we all rush for. We had cheap and abundant fresh cattle milk to buy from their women but today, the story has changed.

Pay attention! The discourse in this book is not targeting any ethnic or religious groups as many have heralded. This is because I have seen Christian and Muslems, Kadara, Hausa, Fulani, Koro, Gbagyi and Igbo been displaced by bandits. Every group is suffering the consequences, and so this book can never mention that the happening in this axis is targeted some specific group of people.

Earlier when this bandit began to rear their ugly heads in Paikoro Local government area, the Police stations of A male and Beni were closed, the officers in those outposts we called back to the divisional headquarters.

We felt this was a calculated attempt to give these hoodlums all the space they need to perpetuate what they know how to do best. I need to mention to you that the same Beni and Amale suffered more attacks than any part of Paikoro Local government.

These bandits usually send an herald ahead of them to announce their coming. And so, in the third week of March 2022, the bandits send a signal to Adunu that they were coming on March 28. We expected the Police DPO to beef up security in the region but his actions weakened our bones when he called off the few police officers in Adunu and the Police outpost was closed.

And on March 28 as announced, the bandits stormed

Adunu my hometown on motorcycles that numbers over 150 carrying 2 or 3 heavily armed persons each. An empty village welcomed them because we all fled to nearby bushes to take refuge. They entered Adunu at about 8:00am and packed at the very frontage of our family resident.

Using Axe, they forcefully broke into some shops where they packed soft drinks, bread and snacks and ate. They packed phones from charging centers, fueled their motorcycles from the local fuel stations (black market), and changed their old motorcycles with the new ones they found in our village.

We all were hiding while people who we believed to be bam, were publicly doing what the will. The security was completely cleared to ensure they had no form of interruption. I speak the truth; I am not lying. Since they made their 2022 debut in January with over fifty (50) attacks, no security back up was ever sent until the March 28 episode where something very funny happened that I will discuss later.

They bandits after eating, they passed to nearby bushes where they rustled innumerable number of Cattles. Yes, innumerable number of Cattle's. They pushed these cattles through Adunu and lodged in the very heart of Adunu for the night where they made house to house and shop to shop raid.

They razed shops and food store of some people. We slept in the bushes while they slept on our beds in our houses, they slaughtered our chickens and pounded our yams. They ate to their feel and trampled over the remains. They entered some houses, on their generators to charge their phones and also played music and held a party in our villages while we prayerfully hide in the bush.

While fleeing from them, some fell into their hands and they robbed them of their phones, money and other valuables. They continued their activities from 8:00am of March 28 to about 9:00am of March 29.

The only time that we saw a form of security aid was on that March 28 when some Hilux (four of them) carrying a very small number of soldiers numbering less than 30 came and headed towards the very forest where the bandits had just rustled cattles. Immediately we saw that, we all came out of our hideout with great shouts of joy for we said at least, these bandits will be repelled and we will not suffer in their hands as at other times.

Not up to 3 hours later, we saw these Soldiers coming back with a considerate number of cattle herds and some motorcycles we believed they seized from the bandits. We thought they had diffused the bandits and were going to remain in the village with us for some time to be sure the bandits make no reprisal attacks on the village but the Soldiers just passed into the thin air back to Minna with the cattle herd before them and the motorcycles on their vans.

In less than 3 hours later, we saw the bandits come out of the same forests unhurt with still many more motorcycles and a great number of cattle herds that outnumbered what the army rescued. Compared to the cattle the bandits rustled, the Soldiers took nothing. It was then that they returned and unlished mayhem to all the villages around.

As the bandits returned in the evening and the spate of their mayhem increased, our hideouts became unsafe for us and my wife and I had to flee, trekking about 10 kilometers (from about 12:00pm to about 3:00am) that night.

Let me say this in summary: inhabitants of this side of Niger state flee the comforts of our homes at least once every week. Schools are closed and our relatives (students) are forced to stay out of school while their counterparts in cities are schooling. Then we ask ourselves this question: will the standards of their national examination differ from the general standard?

They abduct scores of people who are made to help them chase the cattles they rustled to Zamfara state on foot. On reaching Zamfara, these bandits will demand for ransom and each community will tax its household heads to contribute a certain amount to make up for the ransom demanded. In order we pay taxes to the bandits.

Many women had miscarriages and gave birth prematurely while running from them. They caught one of our brothers who was sick at the time and could not run. They removed him from his sickbed, killed him and hung him on their motorcycle and dragged his body on the ground.

They razed houses, razed Churches and Mosques and gave many people permanent disabilities. What a pity!
Contrary to the notion in circulation that the current security instability is aimed at displacing some ethnic groups to establish the Fulanis, I wish to tell you that the Fulanis from the region I come from were not included as

beneficiaries of such a grand plan.

I said this because I have seeing a Fulani man who owned over 200 hundred cattle lose all in one night. He now owns nothing and becomes an object of pity, he goes about begging for jobs to clear farm lands of others for payment.

This unrestrained thrive of banditry dictates "the when and when not to" of many (religious, business, social) activities. We know their hideouts and their normal routes. The government know all these details too but is doing nothing about it.

Lagbe, a village in Munya Local Government area is now the den of this bandits. Bandits in that axis go to its inhabitants and give them cattle to slaughter for them. The inhabitants will prepare them a meal and the bandits will sponsor a wild party with the locals who must be careful to make sure they do nothing stupid. So, I beg you to imagine what is becoming of the young girls of a place where bandits throw a wild party.

Get the summary:
1. Bandits now controls part of the north central airspaces.
2. Security is relaxed in areas with highest susceptibility.
3. Bandits announce their coming, they do not run secret operations.
4. We have never received any form of intervention since January 2022 except the funny one.
5. No public office holder has come to these regions

to bring comfort to the oppressed citizens in such areas.

6. Some of the claims that these bandits are handled with iron hand are false.

7. You are safer being an outlaw than being a nice and decent citizen.

8. At least inhabitants of these hotbeds sleep in bushes, on trees and in hideouts once every week.

9. None of the promise to bring to book perpetrators of heinous acts has been actualized.

10. To get a close reality of the horror, terror and pain of the innocent Nigerians trapped in such places, multiply all the figures they give, at least by 2. Number of people kidnapped, killed or maimed is much beyond what all those outsiders are saying. In sincerity, they are just trying to be decent.

5 CHAPTER

OUR DEEPEST HEART CRY

These are the silent prayers of the poor masses who are helpless in the face of the current situation:

1. How long will this regime reign before we find deliverance?

2. Will our schools be opened again?

3. What shall we eat if these bandits do not allow us to farm (our only source of income)?

4. Are we going to participate in the forth coming general elections (nobody including the people we gave our votes care about us)?

5. They took a good loaf of money to fetch their children who are schooling in Ukraine for fear of attack by Russia but no body care to extract us to safer zones, security is not beefed up and no IDP camp is established to accommodate the homeless?

6. Our loved ones are in their hands, where shall we get money to pay for the ransom the landowners (bandits) are demanding?

7. Who will deliver us from such a regime that employs banditry as part of its agency?

8. Oh God, look upon us with mercy and yet give us a democratically elected administration that run a true democracy — the very democracy that our heroes in the past fought for and paid the supreme price. May our children not grow to see this menace we are seeing today.

ABOUT THE AUTHOR

Galadima Bitrus is an Animal Scientist, a native born of Adunu in Paikoro LGA Niger State. Married to Gift Galadima, they are blessed with one child (O. B. Augustine).

He currently resides in Adunu where he is working to establish a High School (Burning Light College, Adunu).